Audience with Murder

A thriller

Roger Leach
and Colin Wakefield

Samuel French — London
www.samuelfrench-london.co.uk

AUDIENCE WITH MURDER

First produced in a slightly different version by Theatre Maketa in the Theatre Truck at the Edinburgh Festival in August, 2004 with the following cast:

George	Tim Charrington
Sally	Leda Hodgson
Kim	Aimée Thackray
Charles	Darren Cheek

Directed by Hank Turnbull
Designed by Nick Kidd
Lighting and sound by Luci

This version was first produced by Double Honours Productions, in association with Theatre Maketa, at the Jermyn Street Theatre, London, on 21st February 2006 with the following cast:

George	Dudley Rogers
Sally	Leda Hodgson
Kim	Pippa Duffy
Charles	Bryan Pilkington
The Voice of Ken Wheelwright	Colin Wakefield

Directed by Colin Wakefield
Designed by Colin Mayes
Lighting and sound by Luci
Company stage manager Peter Adshead

CHARACTERS

George, an actor, aged fifty-five,
  playing **Gerald**, **Alan** and **Vernon**

Sally, an actress, aged fifty-five,
  playing **Sue** and **Vivienne**

Kim, an actress, aged twenty-five,
  playing **Hannah**, **Kelly** and **Simone**

Charles, an actor, aged twenty-five,
  playing **Sebastian**, **Dean**, **McTavish** and **Matt**

Ken Wheelwright, a theatre producer, voice only

NB. Only the characters **Alan**, **Sue**, **Dean**, **Kelly**, **McTavish**, and possibly **Ken Wheelwright**, should appear in the theatre programme.

The action takes place in a living-room

ACT I   Around 8 p.m.
ACT II   Five minutes later

Time—the present

NOTE ON THE ACTING EDITION

Audience with Murder is four thrillers in one. Only two levels are ever "in play" at any one time, and these are distinguished in the text by different margins, and a vertical line down the left side of the page to clarify where there is an indentation. The reader should be aware of the different levels from the start, but an audience will only become aware of them as they are revealed during the action of the play.

For example:

Sue Could we just read my play? Do you mind?

> **Sebastian** Hallo, Father.
> **Gerald** Sebastian.
> **Sebastian** How's Mother?

Alan And how come he's in through the door the second after we hear the doorbell?

PRODUCTION NOTE

The design for the living-room should be as simple and uncluttered as possible. In the Jermyn Street production there was a sofa L, on which Dean and Kelly sat for the playreading. Alan had his own comfortable chair R, so he was facing the other two readers. Sue sat on an upright chair UC, next to the drinks table to her left. There were two doorways without practical doors UR and UL, for exits to the hall/loo and the kitchen respectively. When McTavish began his interrogation of Kelly in Act II, he brought her chair down C, where it was then conveniently placed for Matt's terrorizing of Vivienne later. Set dressing was kept to the minimum: some of Alan's theatre posters (from his past triumphs with the Prestige Players) on the back wall, maybe a rug or two, and two small side tables for drinks.

MANAGEMENT OF FIREARMS
AND OTHER WEAPONS IN PRODUCTIONS

Recommended reading:

Entertainment Information Sheet No. 20 (Health and Safety Executive). This information sheet is one of a series produced in consultation with the Joint Advisory Committee for Broadcasting and the Performing Arts. It gives guidance on the management of weapons that are part of a production, including firearms, replicas and deactivated weapons.

It may be downloaded from:

www.hse.gov.uk

Or from HSE Books, PO Box 1999, Sudbury, Suffolk, CO10 2WA. Tel: 01787 881165 Fax: 01787 313995.

Home Office Firearms Law: Guidance to the Police. The Stationery Office 2002 ISBN 0 11 341273 8. Also available on www.homeoffice.gov.uk

Health and Safety in audio-visual production : Your legal duties. Leaflet INDG360 HSE Books 2002.

ACT I

A living-room. About 8 p.m.

There are doorways to the kitchen and hall L and R. The furniture comprises an upright chair, UC, a sofa and armchair, a drinks table and two small side tables.

When the CURTAIN rises, everyone is seated in the living-room of Alan (GEORGE), forty-seven, and his wife Sue (SALLY), forty, who are holding a playreading. With Kelly (KIM), twenty-five, and Dean (CHARLES), twenty-four, they are reading "The Play's The Thing", a thriller written by Sue. Alan is reading the part of Gerald and Kelly, Sue's friend, is reading Hannah. Dean's character, Sebastian, is yet to appear

We join "The Play's The Thing" about twenty minutes into the action

> *Gerald, a sixty-year-old surgeon, is enjoying a quiet evening at home with Hannah, a twenty-five-year-old private nurse. They are finishing their bottle of wine after a good dinner. It is about 9 p.m.*
>
> **Hannah** He was the sweetest old man, he really was. But he couldn't manage the stairs, you see, towards the end. So we had to make up a room for him downstairs. Trouble was, the only available space was this tiny utility room. No more than a cupboard, really. Where they used to keep the mops and brushes and buckets and things. There wasn't enough room to swing a cat, let alone nurse a ninety-seven-year-old. Bless him. He didn't mind, though. He was downstairs, where the action was. But I used to get the giggles every time I went in. You see his name was Mr Broome. Albert Broome. Spending his last days in the broom cupboard. It cracked me up.
>
> *Gerald laughs*
>
> It's good to hear you laughing, Gerald.
> **Gerald** Broom cupboard. Oh, dear.
>
> *Hannah laughs*
>
> I could do with a top up.

Sue (*reading the stage directions*) "Gerald pours himself a glass from the bottle."

Alan gets up and pours himself a glass from the bottle

Alan Anyone else?
Sue Alan…
Dean (*holding out his glass*) Cheers, Mr Downing.
Alan Look, I've told you — it's Alan. We've just done a play together, for God's sake.

Alan fills Dean's glass

Dean Sorry. Alan.
Alan Kelly?
Kelly Go on, why not? Thanks, Alan.

Alan fills Kelly's glass

Alan (*to Sue*) Darling?
Sue Could we just get on?
Alan Sorry, sorry. (*He sits. Pause*) Where was I?
Sue "I could do with a top up".
Alan (*finding his place*) Ah, yes …

Gerald Darling?
Hannah No more for me, Gerald, thank you.
Gerald Broom cupboard!
Hannah I've been so lucky with my patients. I've had a couple of cantankerous old sods, but on the whole they've been wonderful people.
Gerald That's to your credit, my darling. Sylvia wasn't always the easiest of women.
Hannah I thought she was lovely. When I think of how she suffered. Particularly these last few weeks.
Gerald I could never have got through this without you, Hannah.
Hannah You'd have managed. A lot of people go to pieces. I've seen it. But I knew you'd be all right.
Gerald Sylvia adored you.
Hannah She was a very special woman.
Gerald I feel twice blest.
Hannah So, when are you going to tell Sebastian?
Gerald Sebastian will be fine.
Hannah Gerald, we've got to tell him.

Gerald All in good time. He's my son. So I decide.
Hannah I mean, we don't have to rush to tell him about us, but we can't
   not tell him about the death of his own mother.
Gerald Look, I thought I made myself clear. You don't know him, I do.
Hannah I've spoken to him on the phone.
Gerald He's a sensitive boy.
Hannah You make him sound about ten.
Gerald He wouldn't be able to cope. I'll tell him after his exams.
Hannah What am I supposed to tell him next time he rings?
Gerald Whatever you told him the last time. Say she's asleep. Anything.
   I don't care.
Hannah I think it's very wrong.
Gerald Hannah. Sweetheart. Family matters. Enough said.
Hannah It's unkind, Gerald.
Gerald (*with edge*) Hannah!

Pause

Hannah What if he just turns up?
Gerald He won't "just turn up". He's got exams.
Hannah So?
Gerald In Norway.

Sue Ding dong!
Alan Dear God.
Sue (*sharply*) Alan!
Alan I mean, obvious or what?
Sue (*reading the stage direction*) "Enter Sebastian, tw" — —
Alan "He won't 'just turn up'." Ding dong. Enter Sebastian.
Sue (*tight-lipped, pressing on*) "Enter Sebastian, twenty-one, Gerald and
   Sylvia's son. He is tall, willowy" — —
Alan Willowy!
Sue "Tall, willowy, and handsome in a weak kind of way. Sebastian is a
   pharmacy student, studying in Norway, and he is unaware of his mother's
   recent death."
Alan We already know that.
Kelly Not all of it.
Sue It's a stage direction, Alan.

Sebastian Hallo, Father.

Alan Some stage direction.
Sue Could we just read my play? Do you mind?

Sebastian Hallo, Father.
Gerald Sebastian.
Sebastian How's Mother?

Alan And how come he's in through the door the second after we hear the doorbell?
Kelly Alan — —
Alan Enter Sebastian, twenty-one, a tall, willowy magician given to making impossibly sudden entrances in god-awful thrillers.
Sue It's a first draft.
Alan Tell me some news.

Sebastian How's Mother?
Gerald Dead.

Alan (*exploding with mirth*) Ha!

Hannah Gerald! How could you?

Alan Ha, ha, ha!
Sue Alan, I'm warning you.
Alan OK, OK. I'll be good. I promise.

Sebastian Dead? But how... ?
Gerald She had a terminal illness, Sebastian.
Sebastian When did it happen?
Gerald Wednesday — —
Sebastian (*incredulously*) Three days ago?
Gerald — last week.
Sebastian Ten days? That's when I last spoke to her.
Gerald Indeed? Well, every cloud — —
Hannah Gerald!
Gerald You keep out of this.
Sebastian When's the funeral?
Gerald The day before yesterday.
Hannah I'm so sorry, Sebastian.

Pause

Sebastian Do I get introduced, or what?
Gerald This is Miss Freebody.

Alan shakes his head in disbelief

Sebastian My mother thinks... thought... very highly of you, Miss Freebody.

Alan (*to Sue*) You're not really calling her Freebody, are you?
Sue Shh!

Hannnah Hannah. Please do call me Hannah. We've spoken on the phone.
Sebastian Yes. (*To Gerald*) I can't believe you kept this from me.
Gerald You had exams. We didn't want to upset you.
Hannah We?
Sebastian What about Mother? Didn't it occur to you she might have wanted me here?
Gerald She didn't seem too bothered.
Hannah That's not true, Gerald.
Gerald You spoke to her the day she died. Did she express any burning desire to have you at her bedside?
Sebastian You just wanted me out of the way. You were always jealous of my closeness to Mother. That's why you packed me off to that poisonous boarding school at the age of eight.
Gerald It was high time you learned to stand on your own two feet.
Sebastian It nearly broke her heart.
Gerald Proving my point entirely. She'd turned you into a right little Mummy's boy.
Sebastian It was your way of splitting us up.
Gerald Rubbish!
Sebastian (*to Hannah*) Did you know she had a first-class law degree?
Hannah No, I — —
Sebastian She was a high-flying commercial lawyer before she married this toe-rag. He made her give it all up when I was born and he never let her go back.
Gerald She didn't need to work.
Sebastian You didn't want her to work. Stuck at home all day you could bully and patronize her to your heart's content.

Alan (*getting up to pour more wine*) God, this is turgid.
Kelly It's good.
Alan The speeches are too long.
Kelly Speeches?
Alan It's a family argument, for God's sake. Where's the cut and thrust? It should really come alive after Sebastian's entrance. All he does is drone on and on.
Kelly Like someone else I could mention.

Alan What?

Kelly Look, I was invited here to read Sue's play, not to listen to you pontificating all night.

Alan It may be news to you, Kelly, but my wife has invited me to direct this masterpiece of theatrical magic for the Prestige Players next season.

Sue And the invitation will shortly be withdrawn, Alan, if you don't shut up.

Alan (*magnanimously*) Very well. Carry on. (*He sits*)

Sue Thank you. (*Pause*) Dean?

Dean Oh, it's still me. Sorry.

> **Sebastian** Stuck at home all day you could bully and patronize her to your heart's content. Just like you used to bully me.
>
> **Gerald** I don't have to sit here and listen to this tripe.

Alan Good one, Susan!

Kelly } (*together*) Shh!
Sue }

> **Sebastian** Nothing I ever did was good enough, was it? (*To Hannah*) The day I told him I wanted to study pharmacy, do you know what he said? He said, no son of mine's becoming a bloody chemist. Well, I'm sorry, Father. I couldn't make it as an astro-physicist. I didn't have the A levels.

Alan Remind me where you did that writing course, darling.

Dean Don't rise to it, Mrs Downing.

Sue You know perfectly well, darling. I studied evening classes at the City Lit.

Alan I hope you asked for your money back.

Kelly Alan!

Alan They clearly taught you sod all.

Sue Write about what you know. That was their advice.

Alan Astro-physics a hobby of yours, is it?

Kelly Can we just get on?

Alan Fine by me. Let's get it over with.

> **Sebastian** Did you know he used to lock me in my bedroom to make me study?

Alan Oh, I get it.

> **Sebastian** He actually beat me once for failing an exam.

Alan It's me, isn't it?

Sue Now why should you think that?

Alan I'm Gerald. How too, too subtle. And you — let me guess — you must be Sylvia. The long-suffering, talented, perfect little wife. You should look in the mirror sometime, dear. You're both brain-dead, I suppose you've got that much in common. That's how you see me, is it? Violent father and adulterous husband. I'm surprised you didn't put in a dead daughter while you were at it.

Kelly (*shocked*) Alan!

Sue You bastard.

Alan Or is that a treat in store?

Sue You utter bastard!

Dean stands up

Dean Look, I think I should — —

Alan You stay where you are.

Sue Dean, don't go. It's all right.

Alan You've got the poor boy confused. What dead daughter, he's asking himself.

Kelly Alan, leave it.

Alan She knows, of course. Thick as thieves, those two. Actually wondered at one stage if they were having an affair. You know, an item.

Sue Don't be ridiculous.

Alan No, I did. Really. (*To Dean*) She'd come home from the hospital full of Kelly this, Kelly that. I was starting to get quite jealous.

Sue She was the only person who showed me any kindness. I needed someone to talk to, Alan.

Alan You could have tried talking to me.

Sue You!

Alan Debbie was my daughter too, you know.

Sue pours herself another glass of wine

Sue You killed her, Alan.

Alan Pour yourself another glass, my darling, why don't you? Get drunk and embarrass us all to death.

Sue You drove the poor girl to her grave with your constant carping and sarcasm. Nothing she ever did was good enough for you. She didn't stand a chance.

Dean Look — —

Alan Sit down, dear boy. Have another drink We still have my wife's sweet little play to finish, starring Gerald, a thinly disguised version of *moi*: bully, adulterer and now, we gather, a child murderer.

Kelly (*to Dean, cutting through the sarcasm*) Debbie was Alan and Sue's daughter. She took an overdose last summer, just before she was due to sit her A levels.
Dean Jesus.
Sue (*quietly*) She was seventeen years old.

Pause

Kelly (*rising to go*) Dean's right. I'll call you in the morning, OK?
Sue No. Stay, please. Both of you. I'm fine, really.
Kelly Are you sure?
Sue Please.

Kelly sits, then Dean

Alan (*beginning to enjoy himself*) Excellent! Then let us waste no more time in resuming the epic. Dean — your shout, I believe. Something about me — sorry, Gerald — beating you to a pulp for failing an exam.

Pause, while Dean finds his place

> **Sebastian** I want to know, Hannah — did my mother suffer? Towards the end, I mean.
> **Hannah** She died quite peacefully.
> **Sebastian** Was she in a hospice?
> **Hannah** No, she died here. At home. That was her wish. I was with her at the end.

Alan "At the end". "Towards the end". You shouldn't repeat phrases like that, you know. It's very sloppy.
Sue Alan!
Alan Sorry, sorry...

> **Sebastian** (*to Gerald*) And where were you when she died?
> **Hannah** He was working. Your father's been under enormous pressure, Sebastian. He needed to get away. But he's been a tower of strength these last few months. To your mother, of course. But also to me, particularly towards the end.

A snort from Alan

> **Sebastian** To you?
> **Hannah** It hasn't been an easy time for either of us.

Sebastian Excuse me. May I ask you a question?
Hannah Of course.
Sebastian What exactly are you doing here? In my mother's house? She died ten days ago. You were her nurse. It's nearly ten o'clock at night. Why are you here?
Gerald Hannah's been a good friend to me, Sebastian.
Sebastian I bet she has.
Gerald What's that supposed to mean?
Sebastian You're sleeping with her, aren't you? You're sleeping with my mother's bloody cancer nurse. You bastard.

Sue (*reading the stage direction*) "Sebastian starts beating Gerald with his fists."

Hannah Sebastian, be careful. You know your father has a weak heart.

Alan Weak heart, eh? Ha! Another subtle parallel. So as to leave no lingering doubt.

Sebastian How long has this sordid little affair been going on?
Hannah It's not what you think, Sebastian.
Sebastian He doesn't usually waste much time.
Gerald Sebastian, that's enough.
Sebastian I'd guess a couple of days after you moved in. Am I right? Screwing the night nurse while the patient's dying in agony in the next door room. Did you ever stop to think what a charming man my father must be? This hardworking "tower of strength"? This dutiful, bastard husband? Don't imagine you're the first. He's always had an eye for the young nurses. Easy pickings in the hospital. For the big chief consultant surgeon. He used to get a hard-on at the mere whiff of a nurse's uniform. It's true. I heard him boasting about it once. Mother knew what was going on. She'd have known about you for certain. I wonder how that makes you feel? My mother was a saint.

Alan P-lease!

Sebastian The thought of you two actually doing it. As she lay dying. You disgust me.
Gerald Offended your delicate sensibilties, have we?
Hannah Your father and I are planning to get married, Sebastian.
Sebastian I always wondered when he'd trade her in for a younger model. She was a stunning woman, my mother. But he's always preferred them young. As you'll no doubt discover for yourself in due course. Mind you, I expect the old pervert's powers are a bit on the wane.

Alan No long speeches, eh?
Kelly Alan, do shut up.

> **Sebastian** Sixty next birthday. He's no spring chicken. Probably needs
> more than a couple of starched aprons to get him going nowadays — eh,
> Father? Don't think I didn't spot the Viagra on top of the bathroom
> cabinet last Christmas.

Sue Still marking the parallels, darling?
Alan Bitch!

> **Hannah** Your father and I are in love, Sebastian.
> **Sebastian** I don't think so.
> **Hannah** Gerald — —
> **Sebastian** He's never been in love with anyone in his life. Unless you
> count being in love with yourself.

Alan This is such bollocks.
Sue Hit another raw nerve, have we?
Alan It's pathetic.
Kelly I'm rather enjoying it.
Alan I don't mean the play. I mean what she's trying to do. It's embarrass-
ingly obvious that the silly cow's written this preposterous load of old
garbage with the sole purpose of trying to humiliate me. God alone knows
what you two simple souls have done to deserve this bizarre form of marital
role-play, but I dare say all will be made plain.
Sue Alan — —
Alan Yes, yes. Read on. I'm beginning to get into this. (*Pause*) Oh, it's me.
(*He has to find his place*) Er ...

> **Gerald** Piss off back to Norway, why don't you?
> **Sebastian** Was there — —

Alan They're not going to like all this language at the Prestige Players.

> **Sebastian** Was there a post-mortem?

Alan We're jumping about a bit, aren't we, old girl?
Sue Oh, for heaven's sake ...
Alan Didn't they teach you about structure at the City Lit? Or were you off
studying brain surgery that week?

> **Hannah** The cause of death was obvious.
> **Sebastian** I'd have insisted on a post-mortem if I'd been here.

Gerald You weren't here.
Sebastian Only because I wasn't told.
Hannah What exactly are you suggesting, Sebastian?

Alan Ooh, that it must have been murder! How exciting!
Sue Alan — —
Alan (*turning the page*) Nearly the end of the scene. I feel a curtain line coming on.
Sue Do shut up!

Sebastian Who stands to benefit from Mother's will?
Gerald She never made a will.
Sebastian That's a lie.
Gerald She died intestate. As her husband her entire estate passes to me under the law.
Sebastian Including the property in Norway?
Gerald I'm hardly likely to risk killing my wife for a couple of mangy acres of Norwegian farmland, now am I?
Sebastian Who said anything about killing?
Hannah Gerald!
Gerald Seb, old son — —
Sebastian You murdered my mother, you bastard! You murdered my mother!

Alan (*theatrically*) Da da!
Sue Curtain. End of Act One, Scene One.
Alan Thank Christ for that. Somebody give me a drink.

Sue passes the bottle of wine. Alan goes to the drinks table to pour himself a brandy

Dean, fancy a brandy?
Dean Not for me, thanks.
Alan Come on.
Dean It's really good, Mrs Downing. That's a great ending to the first scene.
Alan Not bad for a melodrama.
Dean Did they really murder the wife? Gerald, I mean?
Sue All will be revealed, Dean, my love. That's what the whole play is about.
Alan Loath as I am to contradict our esteemed authoress, the whole play is about me. Get Alan — that's the name of the game. And there, my angel, you have singularly failed.
Dean Do you mind if I use your... um...
Alan In fact, I'm rather enjoying myself.
Sue It's straight through the hall. On your right.

Dean Cheers.

Dean exits

Alan Fine young actor, that boy.

Kelly I like him doing the accent. It's very good.

Alan (*filling Kelly's glass*) Could have gone to drama school if he'd had the guts.

Sue If he'd had the money. It costs a fortune to train as an actor nowadays. And they've cut right back on grants.

Alan How come you're so knowledgeable?

Sue He was telling me.

Alan Dean?

Sue The other night.

Alan (*archly*) Oh yes?

Sue At the theatre. (*To Kelly*) We've just done *Who's Afraid Of Virginia Woolf?*

Kelly I know. I'm sorry I missed it.

Sue Alan played George — —

Kelly Naturally.

Sue And he got Dean to play Nick. He's one of Alan's ex-pupils. I told you that. He was very good, wasn't he, darling?

Alan It was a strong cast.

Kelly Didn't you want to play Martha?

Alan Ha!

Sue God, no. I don't act any more anyway. I just do front of house — coffee, programmes, that sort of thing.

Alan All she's fit for.

Kelly (*pointedly, to Alan*) How many thrillers have you written, then?

Dean enters

Alan You don't seriously call this pathetic little effort a thriller, do you?

Dean It's good.

Alan Ha!

Dean But I was thinking ... I hope you don't mind me saying this, Mrs Downing — —

Sue Go ahead.

Dean You said you wanted feedback ...

Alan Spit it out.

Dean I was wondering if it isn't all a bit static at the beginning. I mean, before Sebastian comes on.

Kelly You've got to set the scene, haven't you?

Alan Not for twenty-five bloody pages you haven't.

Sue Alan! Shut up!

Alan You see? She asks for criticism, then she can't take it.

Sue I am trying to listen to Dean.

Alan Sorry, sorry. Dean, love: over to you.

Dean No, well — that was all, really. I think it's good. I mean, I'm interested in all the characters and stuff. And I do want to find out whether Gerald killed Sybil — —

Sue Sylvia.

Dean Sylvia. Sorry. I think what I'm really saying is, don't you need something a bit more dramatic, like a murder or something, before the interval?

Sue We haven't got to the interval.

Dean No, well, I don't mean the interval. But I was thinking: it's the end of the first scene and nothing's happened really.

Alan (*topping up Dean's glass*) Give that man another drink. He's absolutely right. The boy's a born critic. Mind you, he did have a good English teacher. You can't start a play with two characters gabbing away about bugger all for forty minutes.

Sue Fifteen.

Alan It felt like forty from where I was sitting. It's not even as if they're remotely interesting people. Where's the suspense, for God's sake? Little Sebbie's a bit pissed off because Daddy's been shafting the cancer nurse. Big deal. You want at least one body before the first curtain. It's what the audience expects. And these pathetic parallels. You may have cast yourself as the sainted Sylvia, my darling, but that's not going to cut much ice with an audience blissfully unfamiliar with the unattractive, untalented alcoholic you've based her on, now is it? Dean, our resident drama connoisseur — give us the benefit of your considered opinion.

Dean You really can be a bastard, can't you?

Sue It's all right, Dean, you don't have to — —

Dean I think the parallels are very clever, anyway. Gerald's a bully, right?

Alan Quick on the uptake, isn't he?

Dean He bullies Sebastian, just like Alan bullied your daughter — sorry, I can't remember...

Kelly (*quietly*) Debbie.

Dean Debbie. Right. Sorry. Well, he bullied me and all. At school. I was being picked on by the boys in my year, see. Because I was good at music and drama and that. They sent me to Coventry. Called me a pouf. I was twelve and it went on till I was nearly sixteen. I went and told Mr Downing. He was my tutor. And do you know what he did? He laughed. Called me a sneak and a wimp. Told me to stop bellyaching. (*To Alan*) I was twelve years old and you sided with the bullies. (*To Sue*) That's why I think Sebastian's a great character, I really do. I completely believe it when he calls Gerald a toe-rag. I hope Sebastian kills him.

Alan So, if I'm Gerald and you're suddenly Sebastian, perhaps you're planning to murder me. How too, too thrilling. A murder all of our very own. In real life. Now I wonder: is it premeditated or one of those unlikely spur-of-the-moment affairs?

Kelly God, you can be smug when you want to be. (*To Sue*) I agree with Dean. I think you've got him down to a T.

Alan (*to Kelly*) And where does that leave you, my dear? If we're playing parallels? Remind me who you're reading again ... Ah, yes! Hannah the slag.

Sue (*warning*) Alan ...

Alan Who's having an affair with ... (*Mock amazement*) Gerald! Golly! Is there the teeniest hint that Kelly and I might have been having it off?

Sue Don't be ridiculous.

Alan The wife's best friend? Bit of a cliché, but I'm told it does happen. And a far more exciting scenario than Gerald's string of starchy young nurses or, in my case — what would it be? Student teachers? Flirtatious fifth-formers? Well, I put my hand up. Guilty as charged.

Kelly Alan — —

Alan Sorry, does that shock you? Don't panic. I gave fifth-formers a wide berth years ago. Strictly window-shopping nowadays. But student teachers — they're a different proposition altogether. Gagging for it, half of them.

Sue Don't be disgusting.

Alan I find the regular supply of sexy young French *assistantes* particularly inviting. And, boy, do they invite.

Sue In your dreams.

Alan Like someone else I could mention. (*To Kelly*) The wife's best friend. Sitting there as if butter wouldn't melt.

Kelly Alan. Don't.

Alan (*to Sue*) Tell me, my precious, how came you to stumble on the truth of our torrid little liaison? Wifely intuition or a sensational confession by "the other woman"? Dean, love, don't look so shocked. A man's got to play away if he's not getting it at home. Anyway, as affairs go, it didn't register that highly on the Richter scale. Amusing enough while it lasted, though.

Kelly Amusing?

Alan Come on, it was only a bit of fun. I was at a low ebb. Debbie had just ... Well, I needed cheering up, didn't I? My wife was drinking like a fish — —

Kelly She was having a nervous breakdown, Alan.

Alan To think I never noticed.

Kelly Her daughter had just committed suicide.

Alan Debbie was mine too, you know.

Sue Stop it! Both of you!

Kelly Sue, I'm so sorry.

Sue You're the one I feel sorry for. I suppose he asked to see you? Said he was worried sick about me? All he was worried about was the state of his own pathetic libido. You see, I'd talked about you — the only one who showed me any real kindness after Debbie died. (*To Dean*) I was crying the whole time. I thought I'd lose my job. But Kelly stuck up for me. She was my friend.

Alan Aahh!

Sue I bet he played it up for all it was worth: the devoted husband, the bereaved father wracked with grief at the death of his little girl.

Kelly Yes, I fell for that all right. And more.

Alan Ooh, I'm intrigued.

Kelly Your charm, you ... Looking at you now, I can hardly believe… (*To Sue*) But he sure knows how to turn it on.

Alan (*smugly*) Oh, yes.

Sue You fell in love with him.

Kelly (*quietly*) Yes.

Sue I know.

Alan I wondered why she kicked up such a fuss when I broke it off.

Kelly You broke it off?

Alan I've come across some hysterical women in my time, but — —

Kelly I was upset. Of course I was upset. And what we were doing was wrong.

Alan Not what you said six months ago in Brighton.

Sue (*sharply*) Spare us the gory details, darling. You've done enough damage.

Alan (*laid back*) Getting back to this feeble little play of yours — what's it called? "The Play's The Thing" ... Oh! I see! A *Hamlet* parallel. Get it, Dean? To catch my conscience. My wife at her most subtle and oblique. Trouble is, poor old Claudius was a bit lacking in the conscience department. Never a great believer in guilt myself anyway. Whereas my talented spouse here — she was brought up a Catholic, and they've rather turned guilt into a religion, don't you agree? Still, onward and upward. Act One, Scene Two!

Kelly We're not going on with this, are we?

Alan I sincerely hope so.

Kelly Sue?

Alan I'm just getting into my stride.

Sue I'd like to carry on, if people don't mind.

Kelly You're incredibly calm.

Sue Oh, yes. I'm calm.

Alan Then read on, Macduff!

Sue (*reading*) "Act One, Scene Two" — —

Alan Sorry to mix my Shakespearean metaphors.

Sue (*reading the stage direction*) "Act One, Scene Two. One hour later. Gerald and Sebastian are sitting alone with glasses of brandy. The atmosphere is more relaxed."
Alan Thank God for that.

> **Sebastian** I overreacted. Sorry.
> **Gerald** No, no...
> **Sebastian** It was such a shock. Arriving to find that Mother had died so suddenly.
> **Gerald** Her death was hardly sudden, Seb, old son.
> **Sebastian** You know what I mean.
> **Gerald** It was tough on you, I appreciate that. But she insisted you be left alone to finish your finals. I tried to dissuade her. So did Hannah. But she was adamant. She had your best interests at heart.
> **Sebastian** As ever.
> **Gerald** To the very end.
> **Sebastian** I'm sorry I said all those terrible things. And in front of Hannah. I hope you'll both be very happy.

Alan Isn't this a bit of a turnabout? What's come over our little Sebbie all of a sudden? Or perhaps it isn't Sebbie, but his identical twin brother, Eddie, a dental student from Denmark, who's popped in unannounced?
Sue You said you wanted to carry on.
Alan I do. I do. I can't wait to discover what lies behind this amazing change of heart.

Pause

Sue Dean, it's you.
Dean Sorry ... um ...
Alan Keep up, Dean, love.

> **Sebastian** It must have been difficult for you too, Dad. As Hannah said.

Alan Where is Hannah, by the way?
Kelly Alan!
Alan Shouldn't that be explained? I mean, the lights come straight up on Scene Two, and she's completely disappeared.
Sue (*wearily*) She hasn't "disappeared".
Alan Is she dead?
Sue For heaven's sake.
Alan Well?
Sue No, she isn't bloody dead.
Alan So, where is she?

Sue She's in the loo.

Alan Ha!

Sue What's so funny about that?

Alan Being sick in there, is she?

Sue What?

Alan Sick. In the loo. Is she being sick?

Sue No.

Alan Just wondered.

Kelly (*too calm*) Why should she be being sick?

Alan Thought she might be pregnant. (*Pause*) Is she pregnant?

Sue (*quietly*) No. She isn't pregnant.

Alan Thought it might be another of your famous parallels.

Dean (*getting up*) Look — —

Alan (*to Dean, referring to Kelly*) She managed to get herself pregnant, you see.

Kelly Alan!

Alan The silly cow.

Kelly How did you — — ?

Alan She told me. Nothing much gets past my wife. Should have thought you'd have sussed that by now.

Kelly (*to Sue*) So you knew?

Sue nods

Kelly How?

Sue doesn't answer

Alan I imagine you had an abortion? Was it a boy or a girl, I wonder? Did you bother to find out? Might have been another dead daughter.

Sue (*to Kelly*) I should never have told him.

Kelly No, no...

Sue I don't know why I did.

Alan To make me feel guilty. Failed again.

Kelly starts to cry

Sue Hey, hey ... Come here.

Sue embraces Kelly

Alan Excuse me while I reach for the sick bucket.

Dean is putting on his jacket, ready to leave

Where the hell do you think you're going?

Dean Sorry, Mr Downing — —

Alan (*quite drunk by now*) Alan. It's Alan.

Dean I've had enough.

Alan But we're just getting to the good bit. I can feel it. My multi-talented wife is building up to a climax. And that'll make a change, I can tell you!

Sue (*very sharp*) Alan! That's enough!

Alan Oooh!

Kelly The reading's over, Alan.

Dean Good-night, Mrs Downing.

Alan At least tell us what happens, before Mr Sanctimonious Smug here breaks up the party. I want to know why little Sebbie's so amenable all of a sudden, while Hannah the Whore's throwing up in the bog. Who gets murdered, for Christ's sake? At least tell us who the bloody victim is.

Sue (*patiently, wanting to get this over with*) Hannah gets killed.

Alan (*incredulously*) Hannah?

Sue By accident.

Alan (*dismissively*) Ha!

Sue The intended victim is Gerald.

Alan Aha. A twist.

Dean Look — —

Alan Sit down and listen, damn you!

Sue Do stay, please. Just till I've finished.

Dean (*sitting*) OK. But only because it's you that's asking.

Sue Thank you.

Alan (*mock-impatiently*) Well? Spit it out. Kelly and I are dying to know what happens, aren't we, darling? We're in suspenders.

Sue (*tight-lipped*) The new atmosphere of calm at the top of Scene Two is Sebastian pretending to have a change of heart in order to lull his father into a false sense of security.

Alan (*sarcastically*) Aha!

Sue He's made up his mind to murder Gerald by poisoning his drink with a special drug he's brought back from Norway for his mother.

Dean Is that why you made him a pharmacy student? So he'd know all about medicines and that?

Sue Exactly.

Dean Good one.

Alan Bleeding obvious, I'd call it.

Dean Is it some kind of miracle cancer cure?

Sue On the contrary. Sebastian knows his mother's condition is terminal. He's come home prepared to give her the drug in case her pain becomes unbearable.

Dean Euthanasia.

Sue If you like. She wouldn't have known a thing about it. The drug does taste slightly bitter, but it's easily disguised in any ordinary medicine or sleeping draught. In a person as ill as Sylvia, death would have been pretty well instantaneous. And painless.

Dean What if there'd been a post-mortem?

Sue Very little taste. No colour. No smell. The poison's almost impossible to detect.

Alan How frightfully convenient.

Kelly So what would happen in this case — I mean, if Gerald took the drug?

Sue Well, the usual symptoms in a reasonably healthy person — stomach seizures, vomiting and eventual heart failure. (*Smiling*) Pretty horrible, really. But given Gerald's history, death would almost certainly be put down to a massive coronary.

Dean Sebastian would get away scot-free?

Kelly The perfect murder!

Dean Brilliant!

Alan Bollocks!

Kelly But Hannah takes the poison by mistake?

Sue That's right. Her death provides the Act One curtain.

Alan Highly dramatic.

Sue Act Two establishes a totally new style. The play turns into a psycho-drama, with Gerald and Sebastian stalking and tormenting each other. A sort of father-and-son living hell.

Alan Hark at her. Augustina Strindberg.

Dean It sounds really clever. You wouldn't be expecting that at all.

Kelly It's very ambitious.

Alan It's very stupid. Anyway, how come Hannah the Harlot gets to drink the hemlock?

Sue (*patiently*) Sebastian, as we've seen, pretends to be perfectly happy with Gerald and Hannah's engagement. He goes to the kitchen to open a bottle of champagne to celebrate, but poisons one of the glasses.

Alan I take it that Hannah's terminated her extended sojourn in the lavatory by this time? Or does Gerald entertain us to a solo juggling act while his son and heir is dispensing poisoned bubbly in the kitchen?

Sue (*ignoring him and finishing as quickly as she can*) Sebastian returns with the drinks. He proposes a toast. Hannah drinks from the wrong glass and dies a horrible death. Curtain.

Alan Is that it? She "drinks from the wrong glass"? Just like that? For God's sake, woman, do you seriously expect a sophisticated, modern audience to swallow that?

Sue It happens in Shakespeare. Gertrude drinks from the poisoned goblet intended for Hamlet. I've never heard you complain about that.

Alan Pardon me for breathing.

Sue It's more realistic in my play than *Hamlet*, anyway.

Alan Well, naturally — it would be.

Kelly Tell him, Sue. Explain exactly how it happens.

Alan Had a private preview, have we?

Sue Sebastian comes back with the drinks. He hands the poisoned one to Gerald, who is about to take a sip when Hannah explains that it's a tradition in her family for newly-engaged couples to drink from each other's glasses. Sebastian is appalled, but Hannah insists on showing them how the ritual works. They each take a glass, intertwine their arms, swop glasses, kiss, then drink from their new glass.

Alan Excuse me?

Sue Gerald ends up drinking from Hannah's original glass and vice-versa. So Hannah gets the poison.

Alan Am I being particularly dim, or did anybody follow that? It's far too complicated for an audience.

Sue Not when they see it.

Kelly It's not that complicated. We tried it out the other day.

Alan (*to Dean*) Told you!

Sue Don't be so childish.

Kelly Sue, grab a glass. We'll do a demonstration.

Alan God, what have I started?

Sue takes a glass, as does Kelly

Kelly Right, Sue's Gerald and I'm Hannah, OK? Gerald's glass is the one with the poison in it.

Sue (*pointing to her glass, for Alan's benefit*) Poisoned glass.

Kelly and Sue demonstrate, using their free hands for the swop as Kelly explains

Kelly They cross arms, swop glasses — this bit looks a bit complicated —

Alan Telling me.

Kelly It is a ritual. They kiss — —

Kelly and Sue linger over the kiss slightly longer than is necessary

Then drink simultaneously from their new glasses.

Sue So now Hannah has the glass with the poison in it. She takes one sip,

Kelly mimes drinking

and that's enough. She chokes and dies.

Kelly acts choking

Alan Yes, yes, thank you. Very good.

Sue And curtain!

Dean It's brilliant, Mrs Downing.

Sue Thank you.

Alan Glad you stayed for the denouement?

Dean Can I take the script home to finish in bed?

Alan Oh, p-lease!

Sue Sure. Keep it if you like.

Dean I appreciate that.

Alan (*expansively, the perfect host*) One last drink before you hit the road. You'll need one if you're planning to stay up half the night wading through this load of old shite.

Dean Not for me.

Alan Oh, come on.

Dean No, really.

Alan Don't be such a wimp.

Dean (*sharply*) I said no!

Alan Ooh! Temper tantrum! You should never let the sun go down on your anger. According to the drippy vicar at our wedding, anyway. Not that "going down" had much relevance to our wedding night, if my memory serves me right. One large brandy coming up.

Dean Look, I said — —

Sue (*suddenly snapping*) Oh, for Christ's sake, stop bleating and have a sodding brandy!

Dean Sorry?

Sue (*clearing the glasses*) I'll fetch clean glasses.

Sue exits to the kitchen, with Dean's and Alan's glasses

Alan (*calling after her*) We don't need clean glasses, you silly cow.

Kelly I can't believe the way you speak to that woman.

Alan You don't seriously expect me to take this crap lying down, do you? I mean, how pathetic can you get? (*Overacting*) "The play's the thing, wherein I'll catch the conscience of the king!" What did she want me to do? Burst into tears and beg forgiveness for my sins?

Dean You could have been a bit more supportive.

Alan Like you, I suppose. "It's brilliant, Mrs Downing!" "Good one, Mrs Downing!" "Three bags full, Mrs Downing!" Sycophantic little shit. You make me want to throw up.

Dean I happen to think your wife's very talented.

Alan Are you two having it off or something?

Kelly You never let up for a second, do you?

Alan Not when I'm being insulted in my own home, no.

Kelly That's rich.

Alan OK. Tell me what's so brilliant about this theatrical masterpiece, then. Come on.

Dean Well, I thought the glasses business was very clever.

Alan It's bloody ridiculous. As if Sebastian would stand by and let it happen.

Dean He hasn't got much choice. He's as good as admitting his guilt if he tries to intervene to warn Hannah. Anyway, it happens so quickly.

Alan Got it all worked out, haven't you?

Kelly It's dramatic licence, Alan.

Alan And how come you were so up to speed with all that kissy-kissy nonsense?

Kelly I told you. Sue asked me to try it out with her the other day at work.

Alan I bet she did.

Kelly What's that supposed to mean?

Alan Oh, come on. You weren't exactly backward in coming forward when you got to that bit, were you? Talk about a full-frontal smackeroo. Did you manage to do tongues? Quite shocked our little friend here. Didn't it, Dean, my precious?

Dean Jealous, were you?

Alan Ooh! Sharp as a needle! (*Shouting*) Susan! What the hell are you doing out there? Glass-blowing?

Sue (*off*) Just coming.

Alan Not that blowing has ever been one of my wife's specialities, if you catch my drift.

Kelly You are such a disgusting man.

Alan I suppose we shouldn't be too hard on the old girl. After all, the play is her baby. Pity she didn't strangle it at birth and do us all a favour.

Sue enters with two large brandy glasses. Alan's is primed with poison

Enough unwanted babies in the world as it is. (*To Sue*) Don't you agree, darling?

Sue Dean, I believe you promised to join my husband in a small brandy.

Alan Give the boy a double, for God's sake. Here, let me do it.

Sue No, no. You just relax, darling. (*Pouring two large brandies*) You've worked hard enough as it is to make our little *soirée* a success. (*Handing Dean his drink*) Dean.

Dean Thank you, Mrs Downing.

Alan (*aping*) Thank you, Mrs Downing.

Sue (*unruffled, handing Alan his drink*) There you are, my precious.

Alan Thank you, my poppet. (*About to drink*) Cheers-ho!

Dean No. Wait. I propose a toast. To the success of "The Play's The Thing". God bless her and all who — act in her!

Sue

Kelly } (*together, raising their glasses*) "The Play's The Thing"!

Alan (*cynically, raising his*) "The Play's The Thing"!

Dean No. Stop. Sorry.

Alan Oh, God.

Dean Let's do that thing with the glasses. Like Gerald and Hannah.

Sue No — —

Dean It'll bring you good luck.

Sue No. That's just silly. Cheers! (*She drinks*)

Alan (*camping it up*) Oh, yes. Don't be such a spoilsport, darling. It's a simply spiffing idea. Come along, Deany-weany.

Dean No, I thought you and Kelly, like Gerald and Hannah in the play, and me and Mrs Downing.

Alan You and my wife? Naughty-naughty. No, I want you to show me how this scintillating business actually works.

Sue Alan, leave it …

Alan (*to Dean*) Come on.

Dean stands facing him

Now, what was it? (*Sending it up*) Arms crossy-crossy.

They cross arms

Glasses swoppy-swoppy.

They exchange glasses

And lips kissy-kissy.

Dean is reluctant

Sue Dean, you don't have to.

Alan Leave the boy alone. He's got to learn to snog on stage if he wants to be a real actor. Kissy-kissy… Come on, what are you? Some kind of pouf. (*More insistent*) Kissy-kissy — —

Sue No!

Alan Don't worry, darling. I'll hand him back when I've finished with him. Kissy-kissy …

Dean is still hesitant, but they kiss

There, that wasn't too disgusting, was it? And — —

Sue is speechless

— drinky-winky.

Alan drinks from Dean's original glass, and vice-versa. Dean splutters

Bit strong for you, is it, laddie? Go on, get some more down you.

Dean breaks away. He puts the glass down, coughing badly

Sue He needs some water.
Dean I'll be fine. (*He chokes again*)
Alan (*slapping Dean on the back*) Went down the wrong way, that's all.
Sue I'll fetch some water.

   Sue exits to the kitchen

Alan (*calling after Sue*) He doesn't want any bloody water.
Dean (*retching*) I feel sick.

   Dean exits to the loo

Alan Silly sod. Can't hold his drink.

   Sue enters with a glass of water

Sue Where is he?
Alan Gone to be sick.
Sue Oh, my God.
Alan (*to Kelly*) You're very quiet all of a sudden, little angel.
Sue (*urgently*) Alan — —
Kelly Why don't you just piss off?
Alan (*really quite drunk by now*) That's more like it.
Sue Go and see if he's all right.
Alan I love it when you get all fired up.
Sue Alan, are you listening to me?
Alan Come and give us a kiss.

Kelly slaps him

Sue Alan!
Alan It was only a harmless bit of fun.
Sue (*a serious order*) Go and see what's happening to Dean.
Alan You do. You fancy him, don't you?
Sue Alan! Just go!
Alan All right, all right.

   Alan exits

Kelly (*steadily*) What have you done?
Sue What do you mean?
Kelly You know very well what I mean.

Sue I'm sorry?

Kelly gives her a look

Look, am I missing something?
Kelly I don't think you've missed a trick.
Sue I haven't the slightest idea what you're talking about.

Alan enters

Well?
Alan He's out cold.
Sue My God! Is he dead?
Alan Of course he isn't bloody dead. Don't be so melodramatic.
Kelly Shall I phone for an ambulance?
Sue (*violently*) No! (*More calmly*) No, no … It's fine. Alan, help me get him in here. (*Urgently*) Quickly!
Alan OK, OK. But I warn you, he's been sick all over the carpet. It's not a pretty sight.

Sue and Alan exit

Kelly pauses for a moment, works out which of the two brandy glasses Dean drank from and sniffs it. No unusual smell. She dips her finger in the brandy and takes the tiniest taste. She grimaces and puts down the glass

Kelly exits to the kitchen. Alan and Sue enter, carrying Dean between them. He is barely conscious, but groans occasionally

Alan Christ, he's a dead weight.
Sue Get him into the chair. Quickly!
Alan All right. Calm down.

They manage to drop Dean into the armchair

Sue Dean. Wake up. Can you hear me?
Alan Of course he can bloody hear you. He can't answer you, that's all. He's drunk as a skunk.
Sue Water. Where's the water?
Alan (*passing the glass of water*) Look, I told you. Calm down.

Kelly enters. She remains very cool

Sue Dean. Dean, love. Try and drink this. It'll make you feel better.

Dean manages to rouse himself and takes a large gulp. He chokes badly

Alan Overacting again.
Sue Shut up, Alan.

Dean chokes and dies

Sue (*to Kelly*) Did you call the ambulance?

Kelly examines Dean

  Kelly!
Kelly It's too late for an ambulance.
Sue What?
Kelly He's dead.
Sue No!
Alan He can't be dead.
Sue My God! What have I done?
Alan (*to Kelly*) Are you sure?
Kelly Yes.
Alan But he was fine a few moments ago. He was laughing and joking. You
  can't choke on a glass of brandy.

Kelly takes the poisoned glass and pours the rest of the brandy from the other glass into it

Kelly Why don't you have a drink?
Sue No!
Kelly Calm your nerves.
Alan Yes. Give me a drink, for God's sake.
Sue (*pointedly*) Kelly, that's not a good idea.
Kelly I think it's a very good idea.

She hands the glass to Alan

Alan Thank you.
Sue Darling, no …

Alan drinks. Kelly goes to the phone and dials

  What are you doing?

Alan starts choking

Kelly Dialling nine-nine-nine.

Sue But —— —

Kelly (*to the emergency operator*) Police ... Yes ... Kelly Hughes. I'm calling from Nineteen Elm Grove, Datchet ... I want to report two bodies ...

Alan (*choking*) Two bodies?

Kelly Yes. A murder and a suicide ...

Alan What the hell's she talking about?

Kelly As quick as you can ...

Alan What ... ?

Kelly We don't need an ambulance. ... I see. Very well. But please, come quickly ...

Alan What's she bloody talking about?

Kelly Thank you. Goodbye.

Alan What murder?

Kelly You'll see. Won't he, Sue?

Sue What have you done? Are you mad? (*Getting hysterical*) What have you done?

Kelly slaps her face

Kelly No more than you've done already. One murder each. We're quits.

Sue I didn't mean to kill Dean.

Alan (*choking*) Somebody help me ...

Sue It was an accident.

Alan Please ...

Kelly (*turning on him*) Oh, do shut up! You've got about three minutes to live. I should make the best of it.

Alan Three minutes?

Kelly (*looking at her watch*) Sorry, two and a half.

Alan Water ...

Kelly Piss off!

Alan Please ...

Kelly pushes him down on to the floor

Aarrh!

Sue (*shouting*) Leave him alone!

Kelly goes over to Sue

Kelly (*face to face*) Listen. We haven't much time. Do as I say and everything will be fine.

Sue You knew, didn't you? About Dean?

Kelly I guessed.

Sue It was an accident. It was Alan — —

Kelly I know.

Sue I never meant to use the poison at all. I got it from the hospital. Months ago. After Debbie died. But I couldn't go through with it.

Alan Help me ...

Sue So I wrote the play instead. To punish him. But you saw what happened. He used it to humiliate me.

Alan Please...

Sue In front of you and Dean. So I decided. On the spur of the moment. To kill him after all.

Alan Why?

Kelly Because she hates your guts. (*She kicks him*)

Alan Aarrh!

Kelly Just as I hate your guts. In Sebastian's immortal words, you're a toe-rag. You deserve to die. (*She kicks him again*)

Alan (*in agony*) Aarrh!

Kelly Realistic enough for you now, is it?

Alan You'll never get away with this.

Kelly Stand up.

Alan (*choking*) I can't...

Kelly I said, stand up!

Alan staggers to his feet

Tell Sue what you think of her play.

Alan No...

Kelly gets Alan in a half-Nelson

Kelly Tell Sue — —

She wrenches his arm up

Alan Aarrh!

Kelly — what you think of her play.

She wrenches his arm again

Alan Aarrh!

Sue Kelly, don't!

Kelly Tell her.

She wrenches his arm again

Alan It's good.
Kelly How good?

She wrenches his arm again

Alan Very good. It's a very good play.
Kelly That's better. Now, I think you deserve a drink.
Sue No!

Kelly takes the poisoned glass and forces the rest of the brandy into Alan's mouth

Alan (*choking*) No … (*He doesn't speak again, but chokes sporadically during the following*)
Sue Why are you doing this?
Kelly I figured you wouldn't risk a second murder after poisoning Dean. So I decided to do the job for you. Call it another spur of the moment decision. I just had time to work out the consequences a little more thoroughly.
Sue The police will be here any minute. What do we tell them?
Kelly That Dean killed Alan.
Sue That's absurd.
Kelly Don't talk. Just listen. Remember his story about Alan bullying him at school? We exaggerate it. Dean suddenly had this extraordinary outburst, right? Out of the blue. Triggered by the play, if you like. It brought everything flooding back. He hated Alan, so he poisoned his brandy. He knew he'd never get away with it, so he committed suicide by drinking from the same glass. It all happened so quickly we had no time to act. I dialled nine-nine-nine.
Sue "A murder and a suicide".
Kelly Exactly.
Sue (*still panicky*) What about the poison? Dean should have the poison.
Kelly Well done.
Sue I'll fetch it.
Kelly (*producing the poison from her pocket*) You really shouldn't leave dangerous substances lying around on kitchen surfaces, you know.
Sue That's got your fingerprints on it now.
Kelly And yours. That's OK. We took the poison off Dean, right? (*Going to Dean's body with the poison*) It just needs his prints.
Sue What about the vomit? In the loo?
Kelly (*thinking on her feet*) Simple. Dean dragged himself back here before he confessed.
Sue The brandy glasses?
Kelly Both their sets of prints will be on the glasses. Remember? Glassy-wassy, kissy-kissy? It's perfect.

Sue And Alan. What about him? You've been kicking him. He'll be covered with bruises.
Kelly No. Dean's been kicking him.

She turns Alan over with her foot. He groans

Overacting again, darling?

There is the sound of a police siren in the distance. Sue giggles. Alan gives a last gasp of pain before he dies

Sue Come here.

Sue takes Kelly's hands and kisses her gently on the lips. The siren gets louder then stops. A blue flashing light is visible through the "window" in the fourth wall. Sue starts to laugh

CURTAIN

ACT II

The same. Five minutes later

Alan's and Dean's bodies are where they lay, but are now covered with sheets. McTavish (CHARLES), a thirty-year-old police Inspector, is addressing Sue and Kelly

McTavish This is all rather irregular, ladies, and for that I can only offer apology. But there's been a traffic accident this evening down at Gunner's Brook Junction with major loss of life. Its effect has been to sap our vital resources somewhat. Which is why you've ended up with yours truly. According to the rule book no officer is authorized to attend a violent scene-of-crime investigation on his or her own, but given the tragic circumstances of this particular case it was thought improper that you should be left unattended longer than was absolutely necessary. (*His mobile rings: Teddy Bears' Picnic jingle*) Excuse me.

Sue refills her wineglass and offers a top-up to Kelly, who declines

Yes, Guv.... No, I'm at the house now.... Two bodies, that's right.... Both male, one in his late forties, early fifties, the other ...
Sue (*mouthing helpfully*) Twenty-four.
McTavish Twenty-four. ... Yep, understood ... Er, Guv, how long do you reckon? ... Will do. (*He ends the call*) That was the Super. Forensic are on their way, but it could be anything up to half an hour.
Sue Can I get you a drink, Inspector McTavish?
McTavish Not while I'm on duty, thank you, madam. Now, if you don't mind, I should like to establish a few facts.
Kelly Fire away.
McTavish Thank you, Miss er — —?
Kelly Hughes. Kelly Hughes.
McTavish Ah, Miss Hughes. Yes. It was you who made the nine-nine-nine call, I believe.
Kelly That's right.
McTavish Reporting — (*referring to his notes*) — "a murder and a suicide"?
Kelly Those were my exact words.
McTavish Would you care to elaborate?

Kelly Certainly, Inspector. The first victim was Mrs Downing's husband, as you know.

McTavish Only from what you told me, Miss Hughes.

Kelly The facts are quite simple, Inspector. A playreading was taking place here this evening. Three readers: myself, Mr Downing and Dean Ackerman.

McTavish Ah, Mr Ackerman. Our second body.

Kelly Exactly.

Sue (*chipping in*) He committed suicide, Inspector.

McTavish One thing at a time if you don't mind, Mrs Downing. Mr Ackerman was a friend of yours?

Sue Yes. Well, no … An acquaintance … I knew him from the Prestige Players. He was more a friend of my husband's, really.

Kelly Hardly a friend, Sue.

Sue (*hastily*) No. No, I suppose not. Not a friend at all, as it turned out. He used to be one of Alan's pupils. My husband teaches … taught … at St Christopher's. English and Drama. Anyway, earlier this year Alan tracked him down and cast him in the Players' production of *Who's Afraid Of Virginia Woolf?* He played Nick. He was absolutely brilliant, wasn't he, Kelly?

Kelly (*drily*) I don't know. I didn't see it.

Sue He got the American accent spot-on and everything. More than Alan did. I actually wondered whether Alan wasn't a bit jealous.

McTavish Are you implying there was bad blood between Mr Ackerman and your husband?

Sue Oh, no. (*Suddenly switching*) I mean yes. Yes, there certainly was. But we didn't realize until this evening, did we, Kelly? It all came out. In this huge rush. He began shouting and swearing at Alan. About how he'd always hated him. He even started kicking him at one stage.

McTavish Did he say why he hated your husband so much?

Sue Yes, he did. He was bullied at school, apparently. Seriously bullied. Alan was his tutor, but refused to do anything about it. Called him a wimp and told him to pull himself together. Dean must have harboured this deep-seated resentment against Alan all these years.

McTavish (*sceptically*) And it all came out tonight? Completely out of the blue?

Kelly I know it sounds extraordinary, Inspector, but the playreading must have tipped him over the edge. It was all about bullying, you see. And suicide. He just flipped, didn't he, Sue?

Sue It was completely terrifying.

McTavish Tell me what happened exactly. The precise sequence of events.

Pause

Kelly Sue?

Sue No, no. You say.

Kelly Well, after this great outburst he went all calm again. As if nothing had happened. Alan took it in quite good heart, all things considered. Even offered Dean a brandy.

Sue That was when Dean suggested doing the business with the glasses.

McTavish Business?

Sue There's this bit in my play where people drink a toast but end up drinking from each other's glasses. Dean must have poisoned his own glass when nobody was looking, and that was the glass Alan drank from.

Kelly Within a few seconds he was doubled up in agony, choking — —

Sue It was dreadful, Inspector.

Kelly We had no idea what was happening. Sue fetched him some water, but it was too late.

Sue I thought he'd had a heart attack. Alan had a weak heart. He'd been warned to cut down on his drinking.

Kelly Then Dean started choking too. We'd been so concerned about Alan that we hadn't noticed him knocking back the rest of the brandy. He rushed off to the loo to be sick, then dragged himself back here and collapsed in that chair. Just where you found him.

McTavish Poison, you say?

Sue It must have been.

Kelly (*hastily*) It was. He said so, remember? He confessed.

Sue He confessed. Yes.

McTavish So he must have come prepared?

Kelly Apparently.

McTavish Nothing to do with the play tipping him over the edge.

Kelly I tell you, Inspector, he was mental. How do I know what he planned to do and what he didn't?

McTavish You sound remarkably confident about a number of other things.

Kelly We're only telling you what the lunatic boy told us.

McTavish We?

Kelly Yes. "We". We saw it happen. We're the only witnesses.

McTavish And the poison?

Kelly What about the poison?

McTavish I found no poison on the body.

Kelly He gave it to us just before he died. (*She produces the poison*)

McTavish Why should he do that?

Kelly Your guess is as good as mine, Inspector.

Kelly hands over the poison

Don't go licking your fingers now, will you?

Sue starts coughing

I gather it is a wee bit toxic.
McTavish Are you OK?
Sue (*more serious coughing*) Sorry …
Kelly (*passing her a glass*) Have some water.
Sue No, no … (*Still coughing badly*) I'm allergic to tap water. Get me some
bottled. It's in the fridge. Quickly, Kelly, please.

Kelly exits to the kitchen

Sue (*recovering instantly*) Get rid of her.
McTavish What?
Sue I need to talk to you alone.
McTavish Sue, I'm not sure if that's — —
Sue Just do it.

Kelly returns with a small bottle of mineral water

Sue starts coughing again

Kelly Here.

Sue drinks, and gradually recovers

All right?
Sue Sorry. I don't know what came over me.
Kelly You had me worried for a second.
Sue What?
Kelly Well… (*Laughing nervously*) You know.
Sue Ah.
McTavish I was wondering, Miss Hughes …
Kelly Yes?
McTavish Might I have a word with Mrs Downing? In private.
Kelly With Sue?
McTavish Yes.
Kelly Why?
McTavish Only for a moment.
Kelly Of course. (*To Sue*) I'll be in the kitchen if you need me.

Kelly exits to the kitchen

Sue Alistair, I can't tell you how terrified I've been.

McTavish Keep your voice down, for God's sake.

Sue (*embracing him*) Darling!

McTavish Are you mad? (*Shaking her off*) I shouldn't even be here. I could lose my job.

Sue We've done nothing wrong.

McTavish Except that I'm investigating the death of my ex-lover's husband.

Sue Ex?

McTavish Susan, we've discussed this.

Sue How did you wangle it, you clever darling?

McTavish I didn't wangle it. I was the only available officer. Now, suppose you tell me what the hell's been going on. And the truth this time, please, if it isn't too much trouble.

Sue No need to be sarky.

McTavish You don't seriously expect me to believe that cock-and-bull story, do you?

Sue Not for a moment, no.

McTavish What?

Sue It was utter rubbish from start to finish.

McTavish Then I suggest you tell me what really happened.

Sue Promise you'll believe me?

McTavish No.

Sue (*with a twinkle*) Bastard!

McTavish doesn't rise to this. Sue is obliged to take the situation more seriously

OK — —

McTavish The truth.

Sue You remember about six months ago I told you I thought Alan was having an affair? With one of the girls from work?

McTavish Of course.

Sue Well, that was her.

McTavish Miss Hughes?

Sue Kelly. Yes.

Sue waits for McTavish to react. He doesn't

McTavish Go on.

Sue What I didn't know was that he got her pregnant. Promised to marry her and everything. Then he must have got cold feet, because they had this huge row. I mean, really violent: punching, kicking, the lot. She ended up losing the baby.

McTavish You said you didn't even know she was pregnant. How did you discover all this?

Sue Everything came out tonight. In this great outburst from Kelly. I don't think Alan knew what hit him.

McTavish What was Dean Ackerman's part in all this?

Sue Nothing. He was only here for the playreading.

McTavish So there was a playreading?

Sue Of course.

McTavish Ha!

Sue No, she was telling the truth about that. I told you I'd written a play. Well, it has all these references to infidelity and pregnancy, which Alan started getting very sarcastic about, when Kelly just flipped.

McTavish And suddenly, lo and behold, there are two bodies. I'm sorry, Susan — —

Sue Kelly must have come here this evening with the express intention of killing Alan. Revenge, I suppose.

McTavish So she didn't just "flip"?

Sue Alistair, how do I know? The woman's barking. She had this terrific outburst, then calmed down again, just as suddenly. We carried on reading until we got to the bit where the two men drink the toast from each other's glasses.

McTavish Ah. The "business".

Sue Alan was getting more and more sarcastic about the play. We ended up having a bit of a barny, anyway, and decided to call it a day. Alan offered Dean a brandy before he left, but Kelly must have poisoned Alan's glass, because when Dean suggested swapping glasses, like in the ritual, she tried to stop him. But it was too late and he drank the poison … Are you following this?

McTavish Clear as mud. No, go on. I'm riveted.

Sue The poison must have been very strong because Dean started choking straight away and ran to the loo to be sick.

McTavish So, you're suggesting that he was the first, but not the intended, victim?

Sue Exactly.

McTavish Forensic should be able to verify that.

Sue Alan hadn't got a clue what was going on. Just made some caustic comment about Dean not being able to hold his liquor.

McTavish And you had no idea what was happening either?

Sue Of course not.

McTavish But you know now.

Sue Only because Kelly told me. She confessed the whole thing. Straight out.

McTavish Why should she do that?

Sue Just hang on. As soon as Dean's out of the room, Kelly hands the glass to Alan — Dean's glass — and lets him drink the rest of the poison.

McTavish You don't mean Dean's glass. You mean Alan's original one.

Sue Do I? Well, the one with the poison in, anyway.

McTavish Right.

Sue The effect was instantaneous. At first I thought he was having a heart attack. Then Kelly, bold as brass, told me what she'd done. Dean dragged himself back from the loo in a terrible state. I tried to give the poor kid some water, but it was too late. There wasn't even time to phone for an ambulance.

McTavish But you did phone.

Sue Later we did. We dialled nine-nine-nine. At least, Kelly did. And that's when I realized she was serious. The awful thing was, Alan was still alive when she made the call. In fact, I'm pretty sure he shouted out something while she was on the line: "What's she bloody talking about?" — something like that. They keep a record of emergency calls, don't they? You could check.

McTavish We'll check.

Sue It'll prove I'm telling the truth.

McTavish So why all the pretence earlier on?

Sue Kelly threatened to lay the blame on me unless I corroborated her story. I didn't know what to do. It was only her word against mine.

McTavish I don't follow.

Sue She said that if I didn't go along with her story of Dean killing Alan and then using the poison to commit suicide, she'd say that I killed him. I needed time to think. She knew how much I hated Alan. He was a frightful man, Alistair. You know that. But I'd never dream of murdering him.

McTavish goes to the kitchen door

McTavish (*calling*) Miss Hughes.

Kelly (*off*) Yes?

McTavish Would you mind joining us for a moment?

Sue You won't tell her about us?

McTavish There's nothing to tell.

Sue Alistair!

Kelly enters

McTavish Thank you for your patience.

Kelly What's she been saying?

McTavish Well, we know that Mr Ackerman didn't commit suicide, don't we?

Kelly Do we?

McTavish And we know that Dean Ackerman didn't murder Alan Downing.

Kelly Did she tell you that?

McTavish Mrs Downing, I wonder, would you mind … ?

Sue What?

McTavish I should like to speak to Miss Hughes alone.

Pause

Sue Fine.

Sue exits

McTavish places the upright chair c: an interrogation. Kelly sits on the chair

McTavish Now, suppose you try telling me the truth.

Kelly You've already heard what happened, Inspector.

McTavish I want to be quite clear about this. You are telling me that Dean Ackerman turned up here tonight with the express intention of murdering his old drama teacher because ten years ago he was being picked on at school. Am I right?

Kelly doesn't answer

He seemed perfectly happy to appear with Mr Downing in a recent production of *Who's Afraid Of Virginia Woolf?* Their relations appear to have been remarkably cordial. And how very convenient the playreading should contain a little drinking ritual that he could suddenly employ to his advantage. Come on, Miss Hughes. You must think I was born yesterday. You work at the hospital, I believe?

Kelly What of it?

McTavish With ready access to poisons, according to Mrs Downing.

Kelly Very limited access. Sue, on the other hand, she's a registered keyholder.

McTavish Pointing the finger, are we?

Kelly I swear to you, Inspector, I knew nothing about the poison.

Pause

Look, I've known Sue a long time — —

McTavish Less than a year, I think.

Kelly Yes, but we've become close friends. Really quite quickly. She had a terrible personal tragedy — —

McTavish Her daughter Debbie. I know.

Kelly She told you about that?

McTavish makes no reply

I helped her through her grief. She's a vulnerable woman, Inspector. I never imagined that she could hurt anyone.

McTavish Is that why you're protecting her?

Kelly I'm not protecting her, for God's sake. I just ... Look, you're obviously more up to speed than I thought.

McTavish makes no comment

I don't believe that Sue ever meant to cause any harm. All I know is that I was invited to take part in her playreading tonight. Alan was cast as the husband. But he was sight-reading like the rest of us and didn't realize till we were some way into it that Sue had written the part to try and humiliate him in front of me and Dean.

McTavish I'm sorry. You've lost me.

Kelly It was full of parallels between Alan and the character he was reading. Sue had been quite clever, really. Written him as a real chauvinistic shit. A bully, basically. Anyway, Alan started playing up and goading Sue about the play. It all got pretty nasty, with him making snide references to their private life. Even dragging the awful business of their daughter into it. You see, Debbie committed suicide.

McTavish I know.

Kelly She was only seventeen, the poor kid. Sue had a nervous breakdown. That's when I started getting friendly with her.

McTavish And with her husband, I understand.

Kelly I beg your pardon?

McTavish I know about your affair with Alan Downing.

Pause

Kelly Did she tell you I was pregnant?

McTavish And that he beat you up.

Kelly That's not true.

McTavish Never mind. Go on.

Kelly I lost the baby, but I'd already broken it off with Alan. My friendship with Sue was more important.

McTavish Oh yes?

Kelly Yes.

Pause

You may as well know this, Inspector. Sue already had the poison in the house. But she never meant to use it.

McTavish Then why did she have it?

Kelly From before. From earlier. You see, she'd planned … Oh, it doesn't matter. She decided to write the play instead. As a kind of therapy.

McTavish She told you this?

Kelly It's true. But Alan was too clever. The playreading was a disaster. The evening degenerated into a round of mutual recriminations and she must have just flipped.

McTavish Flipped! Now where have I heard that before?

Kelly So she poisoned Alan's brandy. She knew it would look as if he'd suffered a heart attack. But she'd reckoned without Dean, who insisted on acting out the bloody ritual with the glasses.

McTavish The business.

Kelly So Dean died instead. Or, rather, he died first. Exactly as we told you, only not by suicide. After he'd staggered off to the loo, Sue got Alan to drink the rest of the brandy, and that's when I began to suspect what she'd done. All I could do was to call an ambulance. And you know the rest.

McTavish Why did you say "a murder and a suicide"?

Kelly I reckoned the Dean suicide story might hold water, and it gave us time to think.

McTavish But why risk your neck?

Kelly I knew I'd done nothing wrong, and I thought if I could do anything to help Sue — —

McTavish She murdered Dean Ackerman.

Kelly It was an accident, Inspector. If the silly boy hadn't started play-acting he'd be alive now, sitting up in bed with a cup of cocoa finishing Act Two of "The Play's The Thing", God help him. I dare say that what Sue's done is murder in the eyes of the law, but no way is she morally guilty.

McTavish And the small matter of her husband?

Kelly Deserved everything he got, the devious little shit. I'd have done it myself if I'd had the guts. No, I reckon Sue Downing's done us all a favour.

McTavish I'm not sure you'd be quite such a fan if you heard her side of the story.

Kelly I take it I'm supposed to have poisoned the brandy?

McTavish That's right.

Kelly Having come fully equipped to "do the deed"?

McTavish Presumably.

Kelly And having successfully claimed two victims instead of one, I rounded off the evening with a full confession.

McTavish Yes.

Kelly If I'd just committed the perfect murder, why the hell should I want to confess?

McTavish One final question. Why should Mrs Downing allege that her husband beat you up?

Kelly Because she's a lying bitch.
McTavish Why lie about a thing like that?
Kelly It's obvious. To invent a reason for me wanting to kill Alan.

McTavish goes to the door

McTavish (*calling out*) Mrs Downing.

Pause

Sue enters

I shan't be taxing you ladies with any further questions tonight.
Kelly That's a relief.
McTavish But I shall have to ask you to remain here until the superintendant arrives.
Sue I do actually live in this house, Inspector.
McTavish I'm sorry. I only meant — —
Sue I am happy for Kelly to stay here as long as you need her.
McTavish Thank you.
Sue I don't know about anyone else, but I'm parched. Who's for a drink?
Kelly Yeah, go on, why not. Open another bottle.

Sue opens a fresh bottle of wine and pours glasses for herself and Kelly

Sue Inspector?
McTavish No, no. Not for me.
Kelly I think I'll just nip to the loo. (*To McTavish*) That's if I have your permission to leave the room, Inspector?
McTavish Of course.

Kelly exits

Sue Well?
McTavish Come here.
Sue Alistair?
McTavish You are one hell of a gorgeous woman, do you know that?

Pause. It should look as if one of the actors has dried

> But we are half way through the second act of the dress rehearsal of "Foul
> Play". It is 1.30 a.m. and all the theatre staff and crew have gone home to
> leave the cast to finish alone. Vivienne (SALLY), fifty-five, co-producer of

*the play and the actress playing Sue, comes to the rescue of Matt
(CHARLES), the twenty-four-year-old actor playing McTavish and Dean*

Vivienne (*prompting*) "Quickly. We haven't got much time."

McTavish Quickly. We haven't got much time.
Sue Alistair!

Pause

Vivienne Oh, for Christ's sake! (*Prompting, less patiently*) "Come on.
She'll be back in a minute."
Matt Sorry ...

McTavish Come on. She'll be back in a minute.
Sue Then what are we waiting for?

Sue meets McTavish in a kiss

*Matt, breaks away, wiping his mouth, and drops out of character. Vivienne
is very annoyed, but manages to keep her cool*

Matt Sorry, look, I'm really sorry.
Vivienne Oh, God.

*Vernon (GEORGE), fifty-eight, author, director and co-producer of
"Foul Play", and the actor playing Alan, calls out from the darkness of
the auditorium*

Vernon It's all right, Matt, love. Do you want to go back?
Matt No, no, it's fine. Let's go on.
Vivienne Excuse me, it is not fine.
Vernon Vivienne — —
Vivienne I want to go back.
Vernon Darling — —
Vivienne I said, I want to go back. Right back. We need a proper run at
this. (*Calling out*) Simone!

Simone (KIM), the twenty-five-year-old actress playing Kelly, enters

Vivienne We'll go from Kelly's exit. (*Looking out into the auditorium*)
If that's all right with you, Vernon, my love?
Vernon Yes, yes anything. Just get on with it.

Vivienne (*to Simone*) Give us your last speech, dear.

Simone, Vivienne and Matt take up their former positions

Kelly I think I'll just nip to the loo. That's if I have your permission to leave the room, Inspector?
McTavish Of course.

Kelly exits

Sue Well?
McTavish Come here.
Sue Alistair?
McTavish You are one hell of a gorgeous woman, do you know that? Quickly. We haven't got much time.
Sue Alistair!
McTavish Come on. She'll be back in a minute.
Sue Then what are we waiting for?

Sue meets McTavish in a kiss

Mmm! I'd almost forgotten how good you tasted, my sexy little "ex". "Ex", indeed!

Sue kisses McTavish again

Vivienne kisses Matt more passionately than necessary. Matt breaks away again

Matt (*angrily, to Vivienne*) What the hell do you think you're doing?
Vernon Oh, God!
Vivienne Don't you take that tone with me.

Simone enters

A break in rehearsal

Matt The stage direction states quite clearly, "Sue kisses McTavish again", not "Sue plunges her tongue down McTavish's throat and grinds her pelvis against his crotch".
Vivienne It's called acting, darling. You should try it sometime.
Matt It's called sexual bloody harassment. I could have you for this, you know. You and your rotten theatre company.

Simone Matt, no — —

Vernon Matthew, love. We've all had a long and tiring day. Let's not start saying things — —

Vivienne It's half-past one in the sodding morning, Vernon. This is the first, and probably the only, dress rehearsal of your paltry little play we're likely to get.

Vernon Yes, thank you, Vivienne — —

Vivienne And we have never — I repeat never — had a clean run of this wretched scene without the whole creative process coming to a grinding halt.

Matt Creative!

Vivienne The action requires a good old-fashioned full-on snog, right? God knows, we've discussed it endlessly in rehearsals. Discussed it, but never done it. The whole premise of this pathetic apology for a piece of theatre —

Vernon I say, Viv. Steady on.

Vivienne Vernon, will you kindly let me finish! The whole premise hinges on the credibility of an intense sexual relationship between McTavish and Sue. She happens to fancy younger men, that's all. He goes for the slightly more mature woman.

Matt Ha!

Vivienne But we have to show it, Vernon.

Matt Show, yes — —

Vivienne You have a problem with that?

Matt I don't have a problem with that — —

Vernon If we could just get on — —

Matt I have a problem with you.

Vernon Everybody. Please.

Vivienne Oh, do stop bleating, Vernon. (*Too sweetly*) I'm sorry, Matthew, darling. You were saying?

Matt I don't mind having to kiss you as such — —

Vivienne How perfectly sweet of you.

Matt But every time we get to this bit you start coming on to me.

Vivienne Poor, sensitive, little lamb.

Matt (*out to Vernon*) She's been trying to get into my fucking trousers since the first day of rehearsal.

Vivienne You should be so lucky!

Simone Matt. Leave it.

Matt I should have listened to my mate Wayne. He warned me.

Vivienne Don't tell me you know the gorgeous Wayne Strong?

Matt Yeah. I saw that tacky farce you did, and all.

Vivienne Dear, sweet, sexy Wayne!

Matt He had a rather different opinon of you, Mrs King. I dare say you found him very fetching, scampering around the stage in his snug little boxer shorts. But I gather you didn't quite manage to bring it off with him either, did you? If you'll pardon the expression.

Vernon I take it we've all quite finished?

Vivienne Not quite. (*Turning on Matt; harsh and aggressive*) Now you listen to me, young man. You were hired by this company to do a job. You signed up with The Kings' Men to play Inspector McTavish and Dean Ackerman in the new Vernon King thriller "Foul Play". Perhaps you'd care to explain which part of this contract you find hard to understand. No? Then I should point out that your duties do not include making suggestive remarks about the private lives of fellow actors or refusing to rehearse routine business fundamental to the plot. We're not asking you to perform in the nude, for God's sake. Though in your case that might be good for a cheap laugh.

Matt (*suddenly exploding, taking everybody by surprise: a frightening outburst*) Shut up, you stupid bitch! Just shut up! You're so fucking unfair! I've tried to do it, but I can't! You disgust me, you repellent, repulsive woman!

Vernon Matthew, that's enough — —

Matt I feel sorry for you, mate, I really do, married to that manipulative cow. I haven't minded doing your play. Shit! What am I saying? I've been bloody miserable. It stinks. Call it a thriller? It's all talk, for fuck's sake. And as for the so-called sodding ending! It's a joke! Enter one slightly inebriated police superintendant, played for laughs by the ever-versatile Vernon King, to announce he's taking the two prime suspects into custody for questioning. The prime suspects being — wait for it — Kelly Hughes and Inspector McTavish! I mean, do me a favour. Well, you can stuff your rotten thriller, you can stuff your sodding theatre company and you can stuff your job.

Matt exits

Simone Matt. Wait …

Vernon Miss Pringle?

Simone Sorry?

Vernon comes up on to the stage. He is dressed in his director's clothes

Vernon Perhaps you'd care to make a little speech. I believe it's your turn.

Vivienne Stop it, Vernon.

Simone Shouldn't someone go after him?

Vivienne No.

Simone He's very upset.

Vivienne (*turning on her*) I'm very upset!

Simone I'm sorry, I was only trying — —

Vivienne Well, don't. Vernon, are you going to stand there all night like a damp flannel?

Vernon Perhaps we should just call it a day.

Vivienne Bloody marvellous! No dress rehearsal, Vernon, no show. In just under eighteen hours' time there'll be six hundred punters out there eagerly awaiting the world première of the new Vernon King. Will you walk out on stage to tell them it's cancelled or shall I?

Simone I'll go and see if I can persuade him to come back.

Vivienne What a perfect little poppet you are. (*Aggressively*) Well, don't just stand there like a sodding lemon. Get up there.

Simone exits

Vernon You have such a winning way with words, my darling.

Vivienne Cut the crap, Vernon. What are we going to do?

Vernon Let's hope she'll be able to coax him back down.

Vivienne He's not a kitten up a frigging tree. You do realize he's on the brink of a nervous breakdown?

Vernon And whose fault's that?

Vivienne Oh, come on — —

Vernon You just couldn't keep your hands off, could you? The moment he walked into the audition ... (*Spelling it out*) I've seen it all before, Vivienne. Wayne Strong last year. At least he had the good taste to resist your sultry charms. Who was it the year before? Oh, yes: dishy Darren — —

Vivienne Shut up, darling. You're being very boring.

Vernon I've always been aware of your sordid little affairs.

Vivienne For God's sake, Vernon, stop sounding so pathetic. A woman's got to play away if she's not getting it at home. Besides, I always imagined it left you free for a quick frolic with the boys. I seem to remember you going off with Wayne to choose his sexy little boxer shorts. And maybe it's my imagination, or is the "kissy-kissy" moment getting just a tad more torrid than when we first started?

Simone enters

Simone He's locked himself in his dressing-room.

Vivienne What's he saying?

Simone Nothing. He won't speak to me.

Vernon Are you sure he's in there?

Simone (*impatiently*) Of course I'm sure. I could hear him banging about. He's angry, Vernon. He's very highly strung.

Vivienne Tell us something we don't know.

Simone I've worked with him before. He's always been a touchy actor, but I've never seen him as bad as this.

Vivienne I see. All our fault.

Simone I didn't say that. (*Sharply to Vivienne*) Did I say that? You have to put a gloss on everything, don't you? The fact is, you've been far too hard on Matt. He's sensitive.

Vivienne He's temperamental.

Simone He's a fine actor. He sets himself high standards. He gets livid when he can't get things right.

Vivienne I get livid when he can't get things right.

Simone Exactly. And that's half the trouble. (*More calmly*) Look, I'm sure everything will be fine. We've got all day tomorrow. There's plenty of time for a dress rehearsal in the afternoon. If we all keep calm.

Vivienne Excuse me, who's running this company?

Vernon Sounds sensible to me.

Vivienne Thank you, Vernon.

Vernon What makes you so sure he'll turn up?

Simone Because he's a pro.

Vivienne Ha!

Simone Trust me. I know him.

Vivienne Yeah. Thick as thieves, you two.

Simone I told you. I've worked with him. I've never known him let anyone down.

Vivienne He's let us down.

Vernon Viv — —

Vivienne No, I'm sorry. It's simply not acceptable. You heard the way he spoke to me.

Simone And you deserved everything you got. You've behaved appallingly towards Matthew since day one. He had every right to say what he did. What is it with you lot? Just because you've got your company logo on the poster and your name in red letters half an inch high you think you can trample over everybody. Well, let me tell you this, Vivienne King: you once try tongues in our snog at the end of Act One and I'm off that stage and on the phone to my agent before you can say epiglottis.

Vernon Simone, love, do try and calm down.

Pause

Simone OK. I'll give you two a chance.

Vivienne I beg your pardon?

Simone I've got something important to say to you. But you have to promise me faithfully that it won't go any further than these four walls.

Vernon Fine.

Simone Vivienne? (*Pause*) I need your word of honour.

Vivienne OK, OK. What is this?

Simone What I'm about to tell you was told me in the strictest confidence. By Matt. It's very personal. He swore he'd kill me if I ever told anyone.

Vivienne Well?

Simone When he was a lad, not that young — about fourteen, I think he said — his mother was killed in a road accident. He didn't tell me exactly what happened. It was a motorway smash, I think. Anyway, his father was in prison and there was no other family except a grandmother, who refused to take him in. Said she couldn't manage. So he was taken into care. He spent the next three years, till he was seventeen, in a residential home run by the council. Throughout that whole time he was subjected to regular and systematic sexual abuse by a senior member of staff. He never told anyone. No-one ever found out. For years afterwards he felt too ashamed even to talk about it. Then one night we were sitting up late in my digs and for some reason he started telling me his story. He was dead calm, as if it hadn't happened to him but to another person. He described some of it in great detail. The things she did to him.

Vernon She?

Simone The matron. She was in her mid-forties. The "slightly more mature woman". Who just happened to fancy 'em young.

Vernon My God.

Simone When he'd finished he broke down. Lay there in my arms, sobbing. Like a little child.

Vivienne Excuse me. We're being asked to shed tears over this, are we? Most boys of his age would give their eye teeth for three years' practical sex education from an experienced older woman.

Vernon Vivienne, the boy was sexually abused.

Vivienne I bet he enjoyed every moment of it. Set him up for life.

Simone You wouldn't say that if it was a middle-aged man with a fourteen-year-old girl.

Vivienne That's different.

Simone It's not different at all, you stupid woman. He was traumatized.

Vivienne Rubbish!

Simone You don't get it, do you? How do you think he's felt every time you've been groping his arse and trying to stick your tongue halfway down his throat?

Vivienne Oh, for God's sake!

Simone I can see I'm wasting my breath.

Vernon No, no. We appreciate what you've told us. Don't we, dear?
Vivienne Yeah, yeah, yeah.
Simone You promise you won't tell him what I've said?
Vivienne No need, darling.
Simone What?
Vivienne He's heard it all himself.
Simone How do you mean?
Vivienne The show relay, sweetheart. The tannoy's been on all the time. He'll have heard every word of your pretty little speech from his dressing-room.
Simone Oh, shit!
Vivienne (*calling out for Matt's benefit*) Sorry about the tongues, darling. You can look forward to the sanitized version tomorrow.
Simone You bitch! (*To Matt*) Matthew, I'm so sorry. Stay there. I'm coming up.

Simone exits

Vernon Why did you have to go and say a stupid thing like that?
Vivienne She'd have found out sooner or later. Sooner rather than later — (*laughing*) — if he's serious about killing her.
Vernon Well, that's certainly buggered things up for tonight.

Vernon exits to turn off the lighting state and put on the workers, then returns

Come on. (*For Matt's benefit*) Your call, Mr Blain, is one twenty-five tomorrow afternoon — no, I tell a lie: one twenty-five this afternoon — to start a dress rehearsal at two o'clock sharp. (*To Vivienne*) Who's locking up?
Vivienne Simone. Bert gave her the keys before he left.
Vernon Who the hell's Bert?
Vivienne (*as if to an idiot*) Stage door keeper, darling. (*Calling out*) Simone, if I could dare interrupt your therapy session for a moment, I'd like to remind you that you're responsible for locking up.

There is the sound of a heavy door opening off R

Matt (*off*) Good-night, you bastards!
Vivienne Matt?

The door slams shut

He won't have heard the call for tomorrow, Vernon. Go after him. Quickly.

Vernon Oh, for God's sake ...

Vernon exits R

(*Off*) The door's locked. I can't get out.
Vivienne What?

Vernon enters R

Vernon He's locked us in.
Vivienne The little shit!
Vernon I thought you said Simone had the keys.
Vivienne Had being the operative word, presumably.
Vernon You don't mean — — ?
Vivienne (*flaring*) How the hell should I know?

There is a crash off R

What was that?
Vernon Wait there.

Vernon exits R *and switches on the off-stage light*

(*Off*) Plant pot, I think. (*He switches off the off-stage light*)

Vernon enters R

Must have fallen off a ledge or something.
Vivienne Is someone there?
Vernon I don't think so.
Vivienne (*calling*) Simone?

Pause. They are both unsettled

Vernon Right. Keys. If Simone hasn't got them I'll have to give the
famous Bert a ring. If he hasn't gone to bed.
Vivienne Of course he'll have gone to bed.
Vernon (*losing his temper for the first time*) Then he'll fucking well have
to get out of bed, won't he! Where's my mobile?
Vivienne You left it upstairs.
Vernon Don't go away.
Vivienne Ha, bloody ha.

Vernon exits L

Vivienne helps herself to a real drink: a bottle of gin hidden amongst the prop bottles. She drinks it neat from the bottle. Then there are four eerie taps: metal on metal, amplified

(*Startled*) Who's that?

The taps stop

Simone? Is that you?

Three more taps

Vernon?

Amplified laughter. It is Matt, who has a microphone. It is unclear exactly where the laughter is coming from. Throughout the following he speaks on the off-stage microphone

Matt?

The working lights go out: near black-out, or "stage blue". Vivienne screams

Matt (*off*) Sorry, darling. Did I frighten you?
Vivienne Where are you?
Matt (*off*) Sit down.
Vivienne I can't see — —
Matt (*off, angrily*) Sit down! The chair in the middle.
Vivienne (*very scared*) Matthew — —

A spotlight comes up on the upright chair c

Matt (*off*) Sit!

Vivienne makes for the chair and sits down

That's better. I can see you properly now. Wrinkles, warts and all.
Vivienne Please — —
Matt (*off, angry again*) Shut up, you old hag!

Pause

Vivienne What do you want?
Matt (*off*) You'll see.

Vivienne Vernon will be down in a minute.

Matt (*off*) Vernon is safely locked in his dressing-room, my dear. Don't worry. It's his turn next. You first, then Vernon, then Simone. I'm leaving the best till last. (*To Simone, over the tannoy*) I hope you heard that, you treacherous bitch! (*To Vivienne*) She betrayed me, you see. So I've locked her up. Till I'm ready for her. I've got the keys. And do you know what else I've got, Vivienne King? Do you?

Vivienne No. No, I don't.

Matt (*off*) I've got a little penknife. To slash your nasty face. Just in case you ever get tempted to go after any more young boys.

Vivienne Look, Matthew... (*She stands*)

Matt (*off*) Sit down!

Vivienne sits

(*Off*) Don't you dare move. I'm coming down.

Vivienne Matthew. Please. I promise I'll make it up to you. You've been great, you really have. I'm sorry about those awful things that happened to you.

Matt (*off, still a disembodied voice*) Shut. Up.

Vivienne If I'd known before — —

Matt (*off, upset again*) I don't want to talk about it.

Vivienne OK. OK.

Silence for a moment. Then the light off-stage R is switched on so that it spills through the doorway R. Vivienne turns

Matt?

Another light, off-stage L is switched on

Matt (*off, still on the microphone, his voice apparently off* L) I'm over here, Mrs King.

Vivienne gets up and backs away R. The light off-stage R is switched off

Vivienne (*turning*) Matthew! Don't!

Matt (*off* L) I told you. I'm over here.

Vivienne turns again, looking L

Matt enters R with a length of rope. He walks slowly up behind her

Vivienne Matthew? Matthew, please …

Matt throws the rope round her. Vivienne screams

Matt I thought I told you not to move.
Vivienne I'm sorry …
Matt We've been very naughty, haven't we? Very, very naughty. (*Pause*)
Answer me.
Vivienne Yes.
Matt What have we been?
Vivienne Very, very naughty.
Matt Good girl. And we deserve to be tied up, don't we? (*Pause*) Don't
we?
Vivienne Yes. Yes, we do.

Matt pushes Vivienne down into the upright chair and starts tying her up

Matt And punished.
Vivienne Matt, no — —

Matt pulls the rope tight

  Aaahh!
Matt Shut it!
Vivienne You'll never get away with this. Vernon will ring the police.
Matt How will he manage that, I wonder?
Vivienne On his mobile. You're not as clever as you think.
Matt (*producing a mobile from his pocket*) What's this, then?
Vivienne That's not Vernon's.
Matt (*feigning defeat*) Don't tell me it's Simone's.
Vivienne It's certainly not ours.
Matt Why don't you give hubby a little ring? Tell him how you are.

He hands Vivienne the phone

Vivienne He can hear me perfectly well from here.
Matt (*menacingly*) Ring him!

*Vivienne manages to dial Vernon's number. A second phone rings in
Matt's pocket. Matt answers it*

  (*Cheerily*) Good-morning! Vernon King's mobile, how can I help you?
Vivienne Bastard!

Matt Now. Where's my little penknife?
Vivienne Matthew, look. I'll do anything — —
Matt Too late, my beauty, too late. Are you sitting comfortably?
Vivienne (*in desperation*) Please!
Matt Then I'll begin.

He stands in front of Vivienne with his back to the audience, and cuts one side of her face. Vivienne cries out

(*To Simone, over the tannoy*) I hope you're paying attention to this, my little angel. It'll be your turn soon. (*Very angry*) You fucking traitor! (*To Vivienne, still standing in front of her*) How are we doing? Ooh, lovely. Who'd have thought that shrivelled old visage had so much blood in it? (*Cheerfully*) Other side.
Vivienne No!

Matt cuts again. Vivienne cries out

Matt That's balanced things up nicely.

He moves away. Vivienne's face is covered with blood

Now I think we'd better go and fetch hubby. He'll enjoy this. Vernon! I'm coming to get you! No funny business, mind. I've got a knife. (*To Vivienne*) Don't go away.

Matt exits L

Vivienne (*very fast*) Vernon, listen. There's no tannoy on the stairs. He can't hear me. No heroics, but pretend to have a heart attack. He knows you've got a weak heart. Once you're out of the frame, you can take him by surprise.

Pause

Matt (*off*) Get a move on, you stupid old bastard!
Vernon (*off*) I'm sorry, I'm not feeling very well.
Vivienne Vernon?
Matt (*off*) Shut it, Grandma! (*To Vernon*) Move!

Matt enters with Vernon in a half-Nelson, the knife to his throat

Vernon (*feigning chest pains*) Aaah! My chest!

Vivienne Vernon? Are you all right?
Matt (*throwing Vernon down*) I said, shut it!
Vernon (*seeing the state of Vivienne*) My God!
Matt Quite an improvement, don't you think?

Pause

Answer me!
Vernon Yes, yes. A great improvement.
Matt Thought you'd like it.
Vernon (*a sudden seizure*) Aahh! My heart! Get me a glass of water.
Quickly.
Matt Oh, come on. I'm not falling for that one.
Vernon I'm serious. (*Another seizure*) Aahh!
Matt I must say, your acting's improved.

Vernon now seems to be in genuine distress

Vernon Water. Please!
Matt (*picking up the gin bottle*) Gin any good for you?
Vernon No — —
Vivienne He's having a heart attack, for Christ's sake. Do you want to kill
him?
Matt I don't know. Do you?
Vivienne Of course not.
Matt Open wide.

Matt pours a considerable quantity of gin down Vernon's throat. Vernon chokes horribly

Vernon No. Please. You don't understand. This is for real.

A final seizure and Vernon dies. It is a terrific performance

Matt (*matter-of-fact*) He's dead.
Vivienne He can't be.
Matt You don't sound very upset.
Vivienne Of course I'm upset.
Matt How will you manage now, Mrs King, without your wimp of a
husband to bully?
Vivienne Murderer!
Matt Don't be so melodramatic.

Vivienne You knew he had a weak heart. You killed him. That's murder
in the eyes of the law.

Matt Then another won't make any difference, will it?

Vivienne What do you mean?

Matt May as well be hanged for a sheep … (*Calling out*) I hope you're
listening to this, Simone Pringle. Miss fucking big mouth. (*To Vivienne*)
Where were we? Oh, yes … (*He approaches Vivienne with the knife and
holds it to her throat*)

Vivienne Matthew, I'll do anything you want.

The off-stage light R is switched on

Matt Who's that? (*He moves to look through the door R*) Simone?

Matt exits R in search of Simone

*Simone's voice voice is heard on the payphone, off L, deliberately loud
enough to be heard by Matt*

Simone (*off*) Police…. Yes, very urgent…. I don't know the number. It's
the Hippodrome Theatre … An attack. … Yes, with a knife …

Matt enters R

Matt You bitch!

He tears across the stage and off L

(*Off*) How the hell did you get out?

Simone screams, off

*Matt enters, dragging Simone who still holds the receiver and its lead.
He throws her to the ground*

You treacherous little bitch!

Simone I had to tell them, Matthew. I'm sorry.

Matt (*hysterically*) You did not have to tell them. I trusted you. You
promised. You betrayed me. (*He approaches Simone with the knife*)

Simone (*producing a gun*) Hold it right there.

Matt stops, then takes another move forward

I said, hold it!

Matt takes her seriously this time

Drop the knife.

Matt hesitates

I said, drop it!

Matt drops the knife. Simone edges over to kick it away, but allows herself to be overpowered by Matt, who manages to grab the gun. Simone makes a run for it

Vivienne No!

Matt fires and shoots Simone in the back. Vivienne screams. Neither she nor Matt knows that this is a stage gun with blanks. Simone pretends to die

Matt Two down, one to go. So, what'll it be? Knife or gun? Any preferences? I rather fancy the gun. More final. And less messy.

Simone, behind Matt's back, slowly recovers and makes towards the knife, which lies on the floor within her reach

Count me in, my darling, why don't you? One, two, three — bang! Ready? One.

No response

I said, one.
Vivienne One.
Matt Good girl. Two.
Vivienne Two.
Matt Three.
Vivienne Three.

Matt chuckles and deliberately fires the gun high into the air to terrify Vivienne further. Vivienne faints with fright. Matt lines up the gun again

Matt Four.
Simone I'm sorry, Matthew …
Matt (*turning*) What the — — ?

Simone stabs Matt with the knife. He dies

Simone I'm sorry. (*Approaching Vivienne*) My God, what's he done?
(*Shaking her*) Vivienne! Vivienne!

Vivienne starts to come round

It's all right. You fainted, that's all.
Vivienne (*shaken and confused*) The gun. He shot me with the gun.
Simone (*untying her*) They were blanks. It's a stage gun. I figured if I could
make Matt think he'd shot me then I could overpower him when he was
off-guard. I'm sorry it took me so long. Look at you. You're in a terrible
state.
Vivienne I'm alive.
Simone It's all right.

*She comforts Vivienne. There is the sound of an approaching police siren
and a blue flashing light*

Simone The police.
Vivienne So you got through?
Simone Only just. (*Referring to Matt*) Too late for him, though.

The police siren stops

Look, I'm sorry about Vernon.
Vivienne What? No — he's acting. He didn't really have a heart attack.
Unless … Vernon?

They go over to Vernon's body

Vernon, can you hear me?

Banging on the door

Voice Open up! Open up! It's the police!
Vivienne Vernon!
Voice Police! Open up!

Vivienne kneels over Vernon's body

Vivienne My God! He's dead!

Bright lighting comes up

Charles, the actor playing Matt, breaks out of character and addresses the
unseen producer, Ken Wheelwright, who is at the back of the auditorium

Charles So, Ken, what do you think?

Ken (*voice from the back of the auditorium*) I like it, Charlie. I like it. You'll
have to tone down the language a bit. And Sally, darling, the blood doesn't
really read.

Sally Oh. Sorry, Kenny. It's the first time we've tried it.

Ken Never mind. You'll sort it. No, I like it a lot. It'll go down a storm in
Eastbourne.

Charles You mean you'll take it?

Ken Yeah, why not? We can go into rehearsal in a couple of months. We've
got the cast. You know the lines.

Charles (*ecstatic*) Wha-hey!

Kim (*giving Charles a huge hug*) Well done, my darling. I always knew
you'd do it.

Charles My first thriller! I can't believe it!

Ken We'll talk contracts Monday morning. I don't know about anyone else,
but I could murder a pint.

Sally I'll second that. (*To George, the actor playing Vernon*) Come on,
George. You can stop acting now.

Kim George?

Sally George?

Kim George, are you all right?

Sally George?

Charles My God! He's dead.

Fade to black-out

CURTAIN

FURNITURE AND PROPERTY LIST

Only essential items are listed. Further dressing may be added at the director's discretion. Please see the note on page vii.

ACT I

On stage: Sofa
Armchair
Upright chair
Drinks table. *On it*: phone, glasses, bottle of brandy, unopened bottle of wine, opened bottle of wine, bottle of gin hidden by other bottles, corkscrew
2 small side tables
Wine glasses for **Alan**, **Sue**, **Kelly**, **Dean**
Typescripts for **Alan**, **Sue**, **Kelly**, **Dean**

Off stage: 2 large brandy glasses (**Sue**)
Glass of water (**Sue**)

ACT II

Set: **Alan**'s "body" covered with sheet
Dean's "body" covered with sheet

Off stage: Small bottle of mineral water (**Kelly**)
Length of rope (**Matt**)
Telephone receiver and lead (**Simone**)

Personal: **McTavish**: notebook, pen, mobile phone
Kelly: bottle of poison
Matt: 2 mobile phones, penknife, blood sac
Simone: gun

LIGHTING PLOT

No property fittings required

Interior. The same scene throughout

ACT I

To open: General interior lighting

Cue 1	**Sue** kisses **Kelly** gently on the lips *Blue flashing light through "window" in fourth wall*	(Page 30)

ACT II

To open: General interior lighting

Cue 2	**Vernon** exits. Slight pause *Change to workers*	(Page 49)
Cue 3	**Vernon** exits R. Slight pause *Snap on light off R, with light spill through R doorway*	(Page 50)
Cue 4	**Vernon** (off) "Plant pot, I think." *Snap off light off R*	(Page 50)
Cue 5	**Vivienne**: "Matt?" *Snap off workers, change to "stage blue"*	(Page 51)
Cue 6	**Vivienne**: "Matthew — —" *Bring up spotlight on upright chair C*	(Page 51)
Cue 7	**Vivienne**: "OK. OK." Pause *Snap on lighting off R, with light spill through R doorway*	(Page 51)
Cue 8	**Vivienne**: "Matt?" *Snap on lighting off L, with light spill through L doorway*	(Page 51)
Cue 9	**Vivienne** gets up and backs away R *Snap off lighting off R*	(Page 51)

Cue 10	**Vivienne**: "… anything you want."	(Page 56)
	Snap on lighting off R, *with light spill through* R *doorway*	
Cue 11	**Simone** comforts **Vivienne**	(Page 58)
	Flashing blue light	
Cue 12	**Vivienne**: "My God! He's dead!"	(Page 58)
	Bring up bright lighting	
Cue 13	**Charles**: "My God! He's dead."	(Page 59)
	Fade to black-out	

EFFECTS PLOT

ACT I

Cue 1   **Kelly**: "Overacting again, darling?"   (Page 30)
Police siren in the distance, approaching and getting louder

Cue 2   **Sue** kisses **Kelly** gently on the lips   (Page 30)
Police siren louder then stops

ACT II

Cue 3   **McTavish**: " ... than was absolutely necessary."   (Page 31)
*"Teddy Bears' Picnic" jingle from **McTavish**'s mobile phone*

Cue 4   **Vivienne**: " ... you're responsible for locking up."   (Page 49)
Heavy door opening off R

Cue 5   **Vivienne**: "Matt?"   (Page 49)
Door slams shut

Cue 6   **Vivienne**: "How the hell should I know?"   (Page 50)
Crash off R

Cue 7   **Vivienne** drinks from the bottle   (Page 51)
Four amplified taps of metal on metal

Cue 8   **Vivienne**: "Is that you?"   (Page 51)
Three amplified taps of metal on metal

Cue 9   **Vivienne** manages to dial **Vernon**'s number. Pause   (Page 53)
*Mobile phone rings in **Matt**'s pocket*

Cue 10   **Simone** comforts **Vivienne**   (Page 58)
Police siren approaching

Cue 11   **Simone**: "Too late for him, though."   (Page 58)
Cut police siren